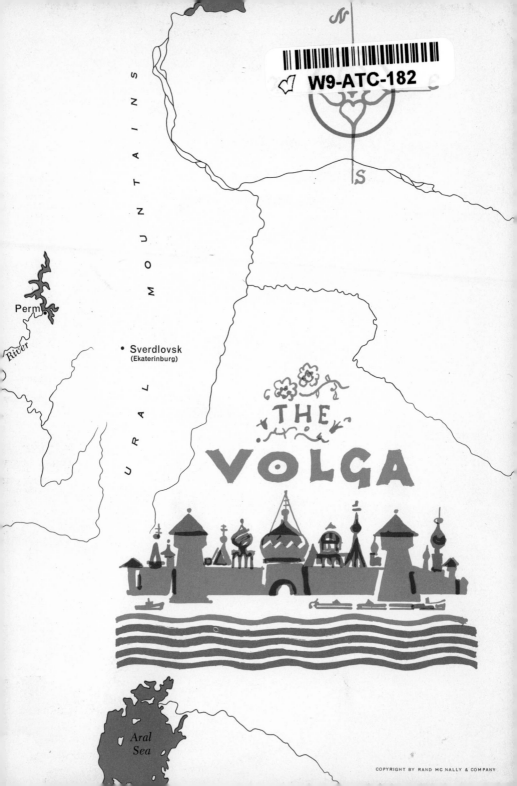

Perm

River

• Sverdlovsk
(Ekaterinburg)

THE
VOLGA

Aral
Sea

THE VOLGA
Lifeline of Russia

By ELVAJEAN HALL
Illustrated by EMIL WEISS

THE VOLGA

Lifeline of Russia

❖

RAND McNALLY & COMPANY

Chicago   ❖   New York   ❖   San Francisco

Dedicated to
Tanya Toothill, Alexander J. Wuertz,
and to the memory of
Edith deCoundouroff

CONTENTS

ILLUSTRATIONS

MAPS

Please Note . . .

There are seven different "systems" for transliterating the Russian language into English. As a result you may find that the spelling of some of the Russian names and places differs in this book from the way you have seen the same words spelled in other books.

The spellings are all correct; the variations come about from the use of different systems of translation.

E. H.

I

MIGHTY RIVER

THERE IS HARDLY a chapter in Russia's story that has not been affected in some way by the Volga River, one of the great rivers of the world, and the longest and most important waterway in European Russia. For hundreds of years it was a "superhighway" traveled by invaders, explorers, and traders. Then, as time went on, it became a "frontier"—comparable in some ways to the Mississippi River and its tributaries in early American history. (See endpaper map.)

The Volga has its beginning in some small springs in the Valday Hills, two hundred miles south of Leningrad. The tiny stream—looking no different from any other tiny forest stream —flows in and out of several small lakes, growing as it twists and turns.

It cuts through changing belts of vegetation—as a spoon cuts through the layers of an ice cream parfait—on its journey of 2,300 miles from the Valday Hills to the Caspian Sea. Like the Mississippi River, which rises in Minnesota and empties into the Gulf of Mexico, the Volga gathers tributaries from time to time and grows wider.

The two largest Volga tributaries are the Oka River, which flows from the west, and the Kama River, which rises far to the northeast. In years gone by—before man started chang-

13

ing the river—the Volga did not carry the same volume of water throughout the year. In springtime it flooded, sometimes spreading out ten or fifteen miles beyond its banks; and in autumn it almost dried up in spots so that navigation was plagued by sandbars.

From its source, until it reaches Kazan, near the mouth of the Kama, the Volga sweeps in a broad eastward arc through forest land which the Russians call the *taiga*. At Kazan, the Volga bends south. From Kazan to Saratov, it winds through parklike, *wooded steppes*, which are forests interlarded with prairies, like much of Minnesota and Wisconsin.

Beyond Saratov, the forests give way entirely to steppes —great treeless plains similar to the American prairies that stretch from the Dakotas to Texas. Strung along a line across Russia, where taiga and steppe merge, are many of the most important Russian cities, such as Moscow and Gorky.

Part of the Russian steppe is rich, black, fertile soil like good Iowa farm land. But the farther south one travels, the drier and more desert-like the Russian prairies become. To the

Taiga and steppe

east of the Caspian Sea, which is shaped like a bean standing on end, the treeless steppes become true desert.

Midway between Kazan and Volgograd, the Volga forms a giant hairpin turn which is called the Samara Bend. Here the river cuts around the Zhiguli Hills that rise to a height of 1,200 feet on the high west bank. On the low east bank the land stretches away in a flat line as far as the eye can see. Between Saratov and Volgograd the Volga flows through unbroken steppe, similar to the dry-grass regions of western Nebraska and the Dakotas.

Below the city of Volgograd, the Volga drops below sea level and cuts through semi-arid, sandy soil and desert until it reaches the Caspian.

A short distance above Volgograd the river forks. The east branch is called the Akhtuba River. It runs parallel with the main body of the Volga for about 330 miles. From time to time the two branches merge as they meander sluggishly toward the Caspian.

It is hard to tell the exact spot where the delta of the Volga ends and the Caspian Sea begins for the river has poured many tons of soil into the Caspian through hundreds of reed-choked mouths. The northern end of the Caspian has become so choked with silt that the water now is only a few feet deep. Russian engineers must work constantly to keep even one channel open for ships.

Astrakhan, on the lower Volga, is not a seaport on the Caspian. It lies many miles inland and the distance is increasing as the Caspian shrinks. Floating docks called "Twelve-Foot Roads" were built many years ago in the Caspian, at the shallow, northern end so that large ships could transfer cargoes to river boats able to go up the Volga.

Since 1929 the Caspian Sea has dropped about seven or eight feet to reach its lowest level in 350 years. This drop is threatening to ruin the Caspian Sea fishing industry. A cycle of warm weather, the diversion of Volga water to irrigation schemes, and increased evaporation on the broad and shallow man-made lakes, created each time a new dam is built on the Volga—are all partly responsible for this new problem. Some Soviet engineers believe the solution will be to build huge reservoirs on upper Volga tributaries so that water can be "trapped" where there is heavy rainfall and channeled into the Volga as needed. Other Russian engineers argue just as strongly that such far-reaching schemes are much too costly to be practical.

A complicated and shallow waterway, making use of small rivers and lakes where possible, links the Volga with the Baltic Sea and the White Sea in the far north. Another canal, about eighty miles long, built between 1932 and 1937, connects Moscow with the Volga.

At one point in southern Russia where the two great rivers —the Volga and Don—come so close together in their twisting and turning that they are less than forty miles apart, still another canal has been built. This engineering feat had been dreamed of since the time of the tsar, Peter the Great, but work on the project was not begun in earnest until 1928. When the Volga-Don Canal, about sixty-two miles long, was finally finished in 1952, the "heart" of Russia at last had an outlet into the Sea of Azov, the Black Sea, the Mediterranean, and the Atlantic Ocean!

Thousands of homes had to be sacrificed so that the canal could be built by Russian labor and World War II prisoners of war. The canal has created lakes, "fenced" in by dikes and dams. The largest of the "lakes" is Tsimlyansk Sea which covers 1,400 square miles. A ship going from the Volga to the Don must be raised 290 feet as it passes through the

The Volga-Don Canal

first seven locks, then lowered 145 feet as it drops through eight more locks to the level of the Don.

This canal was a costly and difficult piece of engineering and it is still so new that it isn't yet known whether its usefulness will equal its cost. To the Russian people, however, it is more than a canal; it is a dream of two hundred years come true.

The Volga is much more than 2,325 miles of river connected with the outside world by a complicated system of canals. It is a river that holds a place that no other river has ever held in the hearts of the Russian people. It is a river of song and legend.

Remnants of the many different peoples whose ancestors entered Russia hundreds of years ago still make their homes along the banks of the Volga. Each group conquered those who had come before, and then in turn was subdued by new arrivals. The Asiatic invaders who swept out of the East in the thirteenth century made their headquarters on the lower Volga and it was several centuries before their power was broken.

Under the tsars, Russia was an agricultural nation. After the Russian Revolution at the close of World War I, the new Communist government began to build industries. In the 1920's and 1930's great attention was given to the development of heavy industry in the Donets-Dnieper area to the north of the Sea of Azov. Even as late as the 1930's, the Volga valley, by comparison, was still an underdeveloped area. It was not until the outbreak of World War II that the cities along the middle Volga suddenly assumed a new importance.

Volga oil was discovered in 1929, but no one at that time dreamed how great the new reserves would be. The Caucasus oil fields in the vicinity of Baku continued to be looked upon as the vital source of Russian oil. Had Adolf Hitler even suspected that the Volga deposits would prove as rich or richer than those at Baku, the whole course of world history might have changed in 1942. Hitler probably would not have divided his forces to send armies against both Stalingrad and the Caucasus. Had he attacked Stalingrad only, it is possible that he might have won the battle instead of suffering a crushing defeat. And—had Hitler conquered Stalingrad—World War II might have had a different ending.

II

SPOTLIGHT ON EARLY HISTORY

LITTLE WAS KNOWN about the river in ancient times. It is said that the Egyptians had heard of it and called it the *Rha*. In the Middle Ages it was sometimes called the *Atel*. However, it was probably a primitive Finnish tribe whose language gave us the word *Volga*.

Some scholars think that early Finnish tribesmen gave names to many of the Russian rivers—all those with names ending in "va," "sha," "ma," and "ga"—as in Volga. Whatever its original name, the Volga River became one of the great water highways of the world and, for hundreds of years, the main route through the heart of Russia for daring invaders.

Nobody is sure how long primitive tribes may have roamed about in ancient Russia. In the dim past, Finnish tribes lived in the taiga. These primitive people lived in constant danger of wild animals and so huddled in groups for protection.

For hundreds of years many ancient tribes advanced and retreated across Russia, crisscrossing the Volga valley as they moved. Sometimes they would join forces with their neighbors; at other times they would slaughter the very people with whom they had formerly been living at peace. Many of these early peoples were Slavic. Later, other peoples pushed down from Scandinavia, and Turkish groups pushed up from the south.

Daring hordes of brutal invaders swept out of Asia from time to time and trampled all who stood in their westward path. One early group, called the Huns, used Russia for a bridge as they fought their way from Asia as far west as France in the fourth century. The Huns struck terror in all who saw them for they had huge heads, deep-set eyes, and

Huns

Vikings

cruel faces. They were broad-shouldered by Slav standards, but had spindly little bowlegs—for they never walked. Huns lived, even slept, on horseback.

About four hundred years after the Huns reached Europe, Viking raiders fanned out from Scandinavia to the southwest and invaded Scotland, Ireland, England, and France. Other Vikings moved southeast and penetrated deep into the heart of Russia. They used rivers for their highways.

Asgard, the mythical city of the old Norse gods, was believed to be somewhere in Russia. No one was quite sure where, but it was always described in Norse mythology as lying "far to the east." Here stood Valhalla, the great hall to which the Valkyrie, who were warrior maidens, carried heroes slain in battle.

According to the *Russian Primary Chronicle*, written by the monks of Kiev in the eleventh century, the Varangians—Viking invaders from Scandinavia—had begun to demand tribute from the Russian Slavs in the ninth century.

The Russian Slavs, say these ancient tales, drove the Viking, or Varangian, raiders from their land. Then—after they were gone—they wanted them back, to put an end to the constant strife that followed their departure.

Ancient legends tell of three brothers who responded to this unusual request and came down from Scandinavia with their followers in 862. One, called Rurik, became the Prince of Novgorod. One, called Sineus, chose Beloozero as his domain, and the third, called Truvor, selected Izborsk. Sineus and Truvor were dead in less than two years, but Rurik lived on and in time gained control of all his brothers' lands. Rurik's daring Slavic and Viking followers then pushed far afield, going as far south as the Ukraine, where they built a fort that, many years later, would be called Kiev.

Around the ninth century, central Russia could be compared to a stage on which a spotlight is trained, the beam shifting first from one settlement to another as centers of activity changed. The first really important "center"—although at that time it was little more than a muddy village of a few huts—was Novgorod.

Up to this time the word "Russian" had not been used. Some scholars think the word is derived from Rurik's name; others argue just as hard that it may have been an eastern Slavic word having no connection whatever with the Scandinavian settlers.

History, legend, and fairy tales were so combined in early chronicles that it is hard to know the truth. Monks used as source materials the stories that had been handed down for hundreds of years from father to son. It is possible that three brothers called Rurik, Sineus, and Truvor never lived. But whether or not three such men with three strange names really did come out of Scandinavia in 862 to rule over the Slavs, millions of Russians down through the centuries believed that they did. Until 1598, all Russian rulers proudly claimed to have "the blood of Rurik" in their veins.

Gradually Kiev, hundreds of miles south of Novgorod, became the more important settlement. Sviatoslav, Prince of Kiev, conquered the Khazars, his nomadic neighbors, on the broad plains to the south of Kiev. In 964, Sviatoslav laid claim to all their lands—even those as far away as the lower Volga. In 968, he made good his claim by sacking the Khazar capital Itil on the lower Volga.

In 965, Sviatoslav attacked another of his enemies, the dreaded Volga Bulgars. They were a fierce Moslem people who made their headquarters near present-day Kazan, where they were held back from their Russian neighbors by miles of unhealthy, malarial swamps, and by a chain of forts that the Russian princes had thrown up for added protection.

Sviatoslav loved fighting. According to the *Russian Primary Chronicle* he traveled light on his raids: ". . . he carried with him neither wagons nor kettles, and boiled no meat, but cut off small strips of horseflesh, game, or beef, and ate it after roasting it on the coals. Nor did he have a tent, but he spread out a blanket under him and put his saddle under his head."

Russian princes were beginning to look to Constantinople, the great Byzantine center, for religious leadership, just as rulers in western Europe were looking to Rome. But Sviato-

Bulgars

slav remained a pagan all his life, although he gradually came under the influence of the Eastern Orthodox Church.

Vladimir, son of Sviatoslav, was the last important European ruler to be a pagan. When the Byzantine emperor in Constantinople asked Vladimir for military aid against his enemies and promised him his sister's hand in marriage in return, Vladimir was baptized, and sent six thousand fighters to help the emperor.

In 990, when Vladimir returned to Kiev from Constantinople with his bride, he ordered his people to be baptized

Christians. In 1037, the first metropolitan arrived from Constantinople to be the head of the Russian branch of the Eastern Orthodox Church.

Vladimir left seven sons when he died, each son ruling as a prince in some part of Russia. Yaroslav, the most powerful of the seven, had been rebelling against his father for some time, refusing to pay the tribute due Vladimir. After Yaroslav's six brothers had either died or been killed, the lone survivor moved his headquarters from Novgorod to Kiev.

III

BATTLING FOR THE VOLGA

KIEV BECAME a most important city of Eastern Europe, and Yaroslav became one of the most powerful rulers of his time.

Yaroslav strengthened his position through carefully planned marriages. He married his sister to the King of Poland, his daughter Elizabeth to Harald Hardruler of Norway, his daughter Anne to Henry I of France, and his daughter Anastasia to the King of Hungary. Three of his sons married German princesses.

Before Yaroslav died, in 1054, he arranged for the division of his lands among his sons—lands that by that time extended to far-distant Volga regions.

Settlers and traders spread out from Kiev, and forts and muddy little trading posts sprang up. Then, in 1233, the "Tatars" appeared—great waves of daring Mongols who swept out of the east from somewhere near Lake Baykal and the Gobi Desert. They arrived without warning.

Under Genghis Khan they had invaded central Asia, north China, Persia, and southern Russia a few years earlier. The first invaders disappeared almost as suddenly as they had come, but in 1236 they were back again, sweeping across the Volga River into Russian territory. The Tatars conquered one after another of the Russian Volga River outposts. They swept on to the west, taking everything in sight.

Batu, grandson of Genghis Khan, sacked and burned Kiev in 1240. Only two hundred houses were left standing in the city that had been the cultural center of eastern Europe. For miles in all directions, the skulls and bones of the city's defenders—men, women, and children—lay whitening on the ground.

For forty years, Mongol hordes, whom the Russians always called "Tatars," were victorious over the Russians. At one

Tatars

time it looked as if they might make good their threat to conquer the world.

The great Italian traveler Marco Polo visited the homeland of some of the Tatars during his travels to the Far East. "They are able to live for a month on mare's milk of which they make a kind of porridge," he wrote. "They are able to stay on horseback for two days on end and sleep as the horse grazes."

Like the gauchos of Argentina, each Tatar had his string of riding horses, sometimes as many as eighteen to one man. As a result, each invader had a fresh horse at his command at all times and could gallop like the wind. If he were hungry and no food was available, he turned to his horse. A quick slit of a vein in a horse's neck, a drink of warm blood, and the Tatar was strengthened for battle again. When there was time to eat in style, he feasted on fermented mare's milk, or *koumiss*, the "porridge" that Marco Polo mentioned.

Some Tatar leaders, or Khans, were crafty in planning their attacks. They did not storm a large town at once. First they would build a wooden wall around the town and then, using the wall as a shield, launch an attack in safety.

One advancing Khan divided his army into "groups of ten." Each unit was told that it must never allow any of its ten members to be captured. If any were, the penalty would be execution for all who were left when the battle was over.

Tatars were cruel. To celebrate one victory over the Russians, an invading Khan laid a wooden floor on the living bodies of his important captives, then crushed them to death as he and his officers feasted on top of them.

Gradually the spotlight of Russian history that had focused so long on Kiev shifted northeast to a little muddy outpost called Moscow, where Prince Yury had first pitched camp in 1147. Years later the spotlight would again shift—from Mos-

Town with wooden walls

cow to the lower Volga and Crimean regions. There the "Golden Horde," as the Tatar invaders came to be called, set up their permanent headquarters.

Tatars could not live at peace with each other any more than they did with the peoples whom they invaded. Hate, rivalry, jealousy—each in turn took its toll at Sarai, their camp on the lower Volga not far from where Volgograd now stands.

In 1437, Ula Mehmet was ousted from the Golden Horde on the lower Volga and stormed north in anger to start his own private "state" at Kazan. His camp became a powerful Tatar center, and the greatest fortress the Mongols held between Moscow and the Urals. There were said to be thirty thousand men, or more, in its garrison.

The crafty Princes of Moscow paid tribute regularly to the Tatar Khans who were their overlords, and even helped them collect the levy from their fellow Russians. It was not until 1480 that Moscow dared openly to challenge the Tatar overlords.

In spite of Kazan's apparent strength, the days of the Mongols in Russia were numbered. In June 1552, Ivan IV, the young Prince of Moscow, led an army of one hundred thousand men against Kazan. Ivan tried to make a crusade of this attack, and began his march toward Kazan with the prayer, "Lord, in Thy name we go forward."

Ivan lost his boats on the river, most of his supplies, and thousands of weary fighters. But the teen-age prince did not lose his courage. Day and night he moved among his men—inspecting, encouraging, bullying. Finally, the stronghold of Kazan fell to his forces and the power of the dreaded Tatars was broken forever.

To celebrate his conquest of Kazan, Ivan had the stone-masons Postnik and Barma build St. Basil's Cathedral near the Kremlin in Moscow. Its moon-shaped domes in many colors and designs have become as much a symbol of Moscow as the Statue of Liberty is of New York.

Ivan's great victory at Kazan opened the door for Russian penetration deep into Asia. It also led to the annexation of Astrakhan in 1566, at that time a great Tatar stronghold near the mouth of the Volga. Almost overnight, with the annexation of Astrakhan and Kazan, the power of Moscow extended to the Ural Mountains and the Caspian Sea. For the first time in history, the Volga had become a Russian river along its entire length.

St. Basil's Cathedral

IV

MURDER AT UGLICH

AS THE WESTERN WORLD slowly pulled out of the Middle Ages, Russia lagged behind.

Ivan IV, the conqueror of Kazan, had inherited the title "Grand Prince of Moscow," when he was only three years old. At sixteen he had announced importantly that he was a "prince" no longer, but a "Tsar," which is the Russian word for Caesar. He was the first Russian ruler to adopt the new title.

At the same time, Tsar Ivan also announced that he wanted to get married. He had no girl in mind, but set out, in a cold-blooded, business-like way, to find a bride.

"I do not want a foreign bride," he said. On this point he was firm. He had seen how few foreign marriages brought happiness or even good foreign relations to rulers. And so Ivan decided, just as the prince always does in fairy tales, to look over all his kingdom for the finest girl in the land. Ivan had many girls paraded before him in order to make his choice, and finally chose one named Anastasia Romanov.

Up to this time the name Romanov had not been well known in Moscow. The Romanovs were originally Lithuanian, although the family had lived for many years in Moscow. Not even the fortune tellers—in whom Russian people

33

of that day put great faith—would have dared predict that a Romanov was soon to become Tsar, and that Romanovs would continue to rule Russia until they were forced to abdicate in the twentieth century.

As Ivan IV grew older, he became increasingly cruel. After Anastasia's death, there was no one who dared check his growing brutality. He had thousands of people put to death; many of them he killed with his own hands. One, whom he murdered in a frenzied fit of anger, was his own favorite son and heir. This left only a feeble-minded younger son, Fedor, to become Tsar when Ivan died in 1584.

As time went on, the real ruler behind poor Fedor was his able and crafty brother-in-law, Boris Godunov, whose story is the theme of Modest P. Mussorgsky's tragic opera, *Boris Godunov.*

Although Fedor was the last of Ivan IV's legal sons, he left another child, Dmitry, who was born to a seventh wife, Marya Nagy, whom the Russians considered a concubine. In 1591, nine-year-old Prince Dmitry was living with his mother in Uglich, at that time a village on the upper Volga.

One day Dmitry was found dead in the courtyard of their home—his throat slit. The people of Uglich would not accept the story that was officially given: that the boy had accidentally fallen during a fit of epilepsy on the knife with which he had been playing. They rioted, and killed the ones who were supposed to have protected Dmitry.

Many people believed that Boris Godunov was responsible for the child's death, for they knew Godunov wanted to be ruler and that, except for Fedor, whom he controlled, only Dmitry stood in his way. Others would not even accept the statement that Dmitry was dead, and swore that the child who was buried must have been secretly substituted for the real prince. They were sure that the true Dmitry had some-

Uglich

how been spirited away and would appear later to claim his rightful place.

Perhaps Boris Godunov did arrange to have the little prince murdered. Perhaps the child did accidentally fall on his knife. No one will ever know. But what is known is that Boris Godunov, in great anger, brought death or banishment to the people of Uglich who had "doubted" him. When his brother-in-law Tsar Fedor died in 1598 without an heir, Godunov at last had his chance to become tsar.

For some time after Ivan IV's conquest of Kazan and Astrakhan, settlement had been encouraged in the new lands opened along the middle and lower Volga. Frontier villages were started that grew to be the cities of Kuybyshev, Saratov, and Volgograd.

So many peasants seized the chance to escape from their hopeless existence in the older parts of Russia that all migration into the new territories was cut off in 1587. However, even the risk of capture and physical torture could not stop the mass flight of thousands upon thousands of desperate peasants during the "Time of Troubles."

The "Time of Troubles" was a fifteen-year period of intrigue, famine, anarchy, and civil war in Russia, to which was added attack from several of Russia's neighbors. It began with the death of Tsar Fedor and did not end until the Romanovs came to the throne.

Boris Godunov had not been ruler long before the "False Dmitrys," as they were called, began to appear. Each man in turn claimed to be the rightful heir to the throne.

The first "False Dmitry," who made his claim in 1604, was a homely, redheaded young man with a big nose and a wart on his face. The nobles had Marya Nagy, the mother of the child who had been killed at Uglich, brought from the nunnery in which Godunov had placed her, to identify this "False Dmitry." They felt sure that she would denounce him as an impostor.

"Look at this man," she was ordered. "Is he your son?"

The woman gazed sadly at the young man before her and her eyes filled with tears. Slowly she nodded. "Yes, he is my son," she said, and clasped him in her arms.

The flabbergasted nobles did not know what to do when they heard her reply, because the real Dmitry had never had red hair or a wart on his face.

The "false" Dmitry married a Polish girl, Marina Mniszech. For a short time after Godunov died of a heart attack, he made a surprisingly good ruler. He was kind and forgiving to those who had opposed him, which makes people think he may really have believed he was the "true" Dmitry. After he was murdered in an uprising by palace guards, other Dmitrys from time to time tried to take his place.

One who looked nothing whatever like the first impostor, being dark and coarse, was also brought before the real Dmitry's old mother. For the second time she was asked to identify a man who claimed to be her son and, for a second time, her eyes filled with tears and she whispered, "This is my son."

Now the nobles did not know what to do. They saw that they would have to think of another scheme to get rid of this bold pretender. They took him to Marina Mniszech, the widow of the first pretender. They were sure that the young widow would quickly denounce the upstart.

But, to their amazement, she did not denounce him.

"This is my husband," she insisted over and over. Perhaps Marina was willing to lie in order to be queen. She bore a son to the "Brigand" of Tushino, as he came to be called, and until the "Brigand" in turn was murdered, swore she was his wife.

The "Brigand" of Tushino's lawless forces captured and sacked many upper Volga towns. At one time they even threatened Nizhny Novgorod and Kazan in the middle Volga area and some of the outposts still farther south.

The "Time of Troubles" finally came to an end. All those who had survived were worn out by fighting. Michael Romanov, a relative of Ivan IV's beloved first wife, Anastasia, was chosen Tsar in 1613 by a general assembly, the zemsky sobor. Teen-age Michael was no one's "first choice" for ruler, but he made a compromise candidate since no one was actively opposed to him.

V

DARING PIRATE OF THE VOLGA

AT THE TIME Michael became tsar, his country lay in ruins. Village after village had either been deserted or burned to the ground. Unburied corpses still lay in empty huts.

While fighting had been going on in all directions during the "Time of Troubles," the people who were able to escape found a new and better life for themselves along the frontier. During the famine of 1601–1603, the flight to the Volga became a stampede.

As the "heart" of Russia was being constantly drained of people, many of the fields that had been cultivated in the days of Ivan IV reverted to weeds. Even in the prosperous Tver area on the upper Volga, one wealthy noble's estate of 2,430 acres had only 256.5 acres under cultivation! Fifty-four of those 256.5 acres were farmed by the owner's own manor serfs; the remaining 202.5 acres were cultivated by twenty-eight tenant peasants from nineteen families. Each peasant household farmed an average of only eleven acres.

This meant that the burden became increasingly heavy on the peasants who did not flee from their homes, because Russian "taxes" were based on the amount of land under cultivation. As a result, those who remained often rebelled against the rulers and took the only possible way to lighten

Peasant farmers

their tax burden—they farmed less and less. Problems connected with the land were to plague the Romanovs as long as they were rulers.

In 1649, during the reign of Michael's son, Alexis, a new code of laws, the *Ulozhenie*, was drawn up, which divided Russians into classes. Under this code most peasants became legally bound to the land as serfs. Traders and craftsmen living in towns also were forbidden by the new law to move from one place to another. The nobility and the church became closed to those who, in earlier times, would have been free to climb from a lower class.

As the Romanov rulers made themselves more and more powerful in the heart of Russia, a strange collection of "refugees" and adventurers became neighbors in the sparsely settled Volga frontier regions. Even Cossacks, who were usually wild and independent, sometimes joined forces with their plodding peasant farmer neighbors and with the wild Tatar tribes of the lower Volga, in their rebellion against the rulers.

The leader of some of the most daring revolts was a Cossack "hetman" or headman, called Stenka Razin. Razin was a rabble-rouser and a part-time pirate. No one ever knew much about his early life, where he was born, or even who his parents were. He was first heard of in 1661 when he was on a mission from the Don Cossacks to the Kalmyk Tatars, then living on the lower Volga. The same year he seems also to have made a pilgrimage to a monastery on the far-distant White Sea! Then Stenka, or "Little Stephen," dropped from sight.

In 1667 he reappeared on the lower Volga, leading a robber band and stirring up trouble. The following year he had a pirate fleet with which he sailed the Caspian, capturing Russian or Persian ships as the fancy struck him, and burning the seaports where he stopped.

Cossacks

In 1670 he went up the Don River, crossed at the spot where, nearly three hundred years later, the Volga-Don Canal would be built, and descended on Tsaritsyn with seven thousand followers. Next, he attacked Astrakhan. He murdered, robbed churches, looted stores. Everywhere he struck, he introduced "mob rule," and called on all who had grievances to join his "army." Pushing up the Volga with thousands of followers, he captured Saratov and Samara. Within three years he held most of the lower Volga.

Songs and legends tell of Stenka Razin's daring, although

many who sing of his exploits know nothing about the true part he played in Russian history.

> From beyond the wooded island
> To the river wide and free
> Proudly sail the arrow-breasted
> Ships of Cossack yeomanry.

> In the first one Stenka Razin
> With a princess at his side
> Drunken, holds a marriage revel
> With his beautiful young bride.

The poem, now set to music, describes how a rumor had started that Stenka Razin had become "soft"—he was forgetting the work of his sword and thinking only of love!

When Stenka Razin heard the sneering remarks of his followers, he trembled with anger. Only for a moment did his eyes rest longingly on the girl at his side. With a roar he burst forth,

> I will give you all you wanted
> Life and heart, and head and hand.
> Volga, Volga, Mother Volga—
> Deep and wide beneath the sun,
> You have never seen a present
> From the Cossack of the Don.
> And that peace might rule as ever
> All my free-born men and brave
> Volga, Volga, Mother Volga—
> Volga, make this girl a grave!

The poem ends with Stenka Razin, in a frenzy from the jeers of his followers, grabbing the girl, lifting her high into the air for all to see, then hurling her to death in the river.

Razin's superstitious followers believed he had magical powers so that neither sword nor bullet could harm him. But a day finally arrived when his "magic" did not protect him. He was defeated in battle near Simbirsk in 1671 and, wounded, fled toward the Don. There he was captured and taken to Moscow.

"Put him to a terrible death," Tsar Alexis ordered.

Stenka Razin was tortured and then quartered alive. With Razin gone, the Tsar was able to crush the Volga uprisings. Thousands of those who had joined the daring Cossack's band were hung, or quartered, or beaten to death.

VI

FLIGHT OF THE VOLGA KALMYKS

RUSSIA WAS STILL a medieval nation when Peter I, who would later be known as Peter the Great, became tsar in 1682. He was almost seven feet tall, and was strong, energetic, and rough. Peter was the first tsar ever to travel abroad. He saw how the western world looked and he liked it. He decided that he wanted Russia to be a western nation instead of an eastern one, and built what he called his "window on the West"—the beautiful city of St. Petersburg.

The spot Peter picked for his new city was low and marshy and required the filling in of land. He decreed that everybody going there must bring with him some stones for the task. Peter was not above doing hard manual labor and worked side-by-side with serfs and artisans whom he forced into building his new city.

Peter knew a smattering of many trades for he had been a curious boy and liked to work with his hands. Unfortunately, he had little formal schooling and realized as he grew older how much he had lost. Many years later, his daughter Elizabeth told how her father would watch her as a school girl with her nose in her books and say he wished there had been someone to make him do the same.

Peter's lack of education proved a handicap during his

entire lifetime. He wanted to develop his country and make wise decisions, but he needed more knowledge of history, economics, commerce, and government. Shipbuilding and "playing war" with toy soldiers as a boy had not been the best training for a tsar!

As Peter worked to develop Russia along western lines, he found that he needed more and more money. To get money he taxed, and the taxes were hardest on the peasants. Some escaped the tax collectors by "hiding out" in the miles and miles of dense woods that blanketed northern Russia. Sometimes whole villages ran away—the people fleeing to the Volga frontier lands just as people had done a hundred years earlier during the "Time of Troubles." Flight to Volga lands continued all during Peter's reign in spite of severe punishment for those who were caught.

When Peter the Great died, in 1725, he was followed in rapid succession by his widow, the peasant girl Catherine I; his grandson Peter II, who died of smallpox; and Anna, daughter of his half-brother Ivan V. Anna named a year-old baby, who was her grandnephew, to succeed her as Ivan VI.

This plan of succession was upset by Elizabeth, the daughter of Peter the Great and his wife, Catherine. Elizabeth seized the throne and had the baby Ivan hidden away in a secret cell in a fortress for the rest of his life.

Elizabeth then named her own feeble and slow-witted nephew as her heir and had him brought from his home in Holstein to the Russian Court. She changed his name to Peter and had him married to a fifteen-year-old German princess, Sophia of Anhalt-Zerbst, who had been invited to visit at the Russian Court.

Sophia wanted more than anything in the world to be tsarina and so she gladly changed her name to Catherine, her religion from Protestant to Russian Orthodox, and her language from German to Russian. But she found that she was marrying a man who hated her, and who snubbed her in every way he could.

When Peter finally became Tsar Peter III upon the death of Elizabeth many years later, his wife's friends at Court plotted his murder. Once they had Peter out of the way, the driving, ambitious widow managed to get herself crowned Empress of Russia and reigned for thirty-four years as Catherine II.

Catherine the Great, as Catherine II is often called, looked to Germany at times, which is not surprising, since Germany was her native land. During her reign, thousands of German colonists were invited by the Russian government to fill in the still sparsely settled lands in southern Russia.

There was no real need to "import" German settlers as there were thousands of Russian people who would have liked the chance to move into the Volga, Don, and Dnieper River valleys. If Russian peasants had been allowed to do so, they would have stampeded to southern "frontiers" from all parts of old Russia. Unfortunately for the Russians, the old laws, prohibiting the free movement of Russian peasants from the land on which they were born, were still in effect.

A great many of Catherine's new German communities were established in the middle Volga region, especially around Saratov, and at Marx and Engels—towns almost directly across the Volga from Saratov.

So many descendants of these German settlers still lived along this stretch of the Volga after the first World War that a German Volga Autonomous Soviet Socialist Republic was formed as one of the units of the U.S.S.R.

During World War II, the Soviet government accused its Volga Germans of collaborating with Hitler's forces during the German invasion of Russia, or at least of being sympathetic toward the German cause. Without advance warning, the Soviet authorities rounded up the Volga Germans in 1941 and took them from their homes—to where, no one knew!

For years the outside world tried in vain to learn their fate. More than twenty years went by before it was discovered that survivors of the forced evacuation were living in the area around Sverdlovsk, a Siberian city known as Ekaterinburg in the days of the tsars.

In 1762, the first year of Catherine the Great's reign, the Russian nobility won their release from "service" owed to the tsar. This was the obligation that had been used for many years to justify enslaving the peasants living on their lands. Lessening the burden on the nobility unfortunately did not help the peasants. The nobles were allowed to keep both land and serfs, even though the excuse for "freezing" peasants to the land no longer existed.

Catherine created thousands of new serfs, for she gave state lands to her favorites and included in her gifts all the human beings living on the land. Although the Russian serfs were not called slaves, in most ways they lived a life of slavery, for they were bound, not to the land but to their master. They could be sold or traded or rented like animals—or forced to do whatever work their master desired.

In the seven hundred years that had passed since Yaroslav the Wise was Prince of Kiev, life had grown more bitter and frustrating for most of the Russian people. A lucky few had managed to achieve leisure and wealth and copied the way of the West as they saw it through Peter's "window." But for most of the Russians, life grew increasingly bleak under the Romanovs. This bitterness led to many uprisings.

One of the strangest "revolts" against the Russian government came in Catherine's time and was not the usual type of uprising but a mass escape from the country. It is known as the flight of the Volga Kalmyks.

On the fifth of January, 1771, Volga Kalmyks, numbering half a million people, with their flocks and herds, began a four-thousand-mile migration out of Russia.

More than one hundred and fifty years earlier, their Torgut Tatar ancestors, a forest tribe of Mongol people in western China, had left their Asiatic homeland and settled on the banks of the Volga. When the Russian government in 1770 opposed the claims of Zebek-Dorchi, who wanted to be Khan of the Kalmyks, he persuaded his people to leave their home on the lower Volga and return to China where they would be able to live beyond Russian control.

Since these Tatars were Buddhists, they appealed to the Great Lama of Tibet, their spirtual leader, for advice. The Lama set the fifth of January for the departure date, so that those living on the west bank of the Volga would be able to cross to the eastern side, for even the lower Volga would be frozen at that time.

On the morning of January fifth, Kalmyk wagon and camel caravans started to move, approximately twenty thousand setting out at a time. Each group scorched the earth behind it so the hated Russians would fall heir to nothing. The Kalmyks burned everything they could not carry with them—personal possessions, the palace of the Khan, all the buildings in a district covering ten thousand square miles!

Seldom have people endured the hardships the Kalmyks faced on their long journey "home" to a China they had never known, for they were viciously attacked along the way by the tribes through whose lands they had to pass. Even more dangerous than the nomads who attacked them was the remorseless, ever-present, enemy—cold. On many a morning, bodies would be found frozen just as the people had

Volga Kalmyks

sat huddled in a circle around a tiny campfire the night before.

When warm weather came, the Kalmyks had covered two thousand miles, but two hundred and fifty thousand people had already died along the way. All livestock except camels had perished and there were still two thousand miles to go! A trail of skeletons marked their route.

Ch'ien Lung, emperor of China, heard of their flight across the desert steppes with the Bashkirs nipping at their heels. He sent rescuers out to meet them, but the rescuers arrived too late. On September 8, 1771 they found a battle to the death was being fought at the edge of the Gobi Desert. The Chinese drove back the Bashkirs and placed a monument at Ily so that men would not forget either the place of the massacre or its date.

Not all the Kalmyks along the lower Volga started the death march back to their Asian homeland in 1771. Remnants of the Kalmyk tribes remained in Russia, and their descendants make up the Kalmyk Autonomous Soviet Socialist Republic of the U.S.S.R. The capital is Elista, or Stepnoi, a city on the dry steppe land to the west of Astrakhan. Today the Kalmyks are the only Buddhist group in Russia.

During World War II, some of the Kalmyks fled with the retreating German armies that had been trying to capture the lower Volga and the rich oil fields of the Caucasus. After the war, a few of these Kalmyks eventually arrived in the United States as refugees and settled in New Jersey.

Kalmyks who did not join the Germans disappeared— transported by the Soviet government in 1943 to some place deep in Asia. After the death of Joseph Stalin, the Kalmyk people, who had been removed from their homes in 1943, were returned to their desert-like steppes on the lower Volga, which has again been named an autonomous district within the U.S.S.R.

VII

LAST OF THE TSARS

ALTHOUGH THE RUSSIAN TSARS were sometimes called "Little Father," this was not always a term of real affection, for many of them were feared and hated.

Catherine the Great's son Paul was murdered. His son, handsome and well-meaning Alexander I, died under mysterious circumstances that may have been suicide or murder. He was succeeded on the throne by a despotic younger brother, Nicholas I, who considered that his subjects existed only to serve his interests.

Alexander II, son of Nicholas, became emperor in 1855 and showed greater concern for the well-being of his subjects than any other nineteenth-century tsar had shown. It was Alexander II who freed the fifty-two million Russian serfs in 1861—about the same time that four million Negro slaves in the United States were gaining their freedom.

Alexander II died a horrible death in 1881, when a bomb thrown at him exploded at his feet. Six years later an unsuccessful attempt was made to murder his son, Alexander III. One of the five university students executed for the attempt was Alexander Ulyanov, whose father had been a school official at Simbirsk.

Alexander's execution brought disgrace to the Ulyanov family. It was only with the help of his father's friends that Alexander's younger brother, Vladimir Ilyich Ulyanov, was admitted to the University of Kazan. He did not remain long, as he was expelled in a few months for plotting to overthrow the government. He went to Samara, where the Ulyanov family owned property, and studied there independently. After he had passed the law examinations at the University of St. Petersburg, he settled down to the practice of law in Samara.

In 1897 Ulyanov was exiled to Siberia for his revolutionary activities, a common punishment for political crimes before World War I. After this period of exile was over, Ulyanov was given permission to leave Russia, and he lived abroad for many years. It was while he was away from Russia that the world began to hear of him as "N. Lenin," his assumed name.

In 1903, when the revolutionists met in London—for they did not dare to hold large meetings in Russia—they could not agree among themselves on their aims and, consequently, split into two groups. One group was the majority, or "Bolsheviks." The other group, much more moderate than the Bolsheviks, was the minority, or "Mensheviks."

While these two groups were plotting and planning, both inside Russia and abroad, strange events were also taking place in the tsar's world.

In 1894, the tsar, Nicholas II, son of Alexander III, had married the beautiful German Princess Alix of Hesse-Darmstadt, one of the favorite granddaughters of Queen Victoria of England.

Alexandra, as she was called in Russia, bore the tsar four daughters and one son. At first the little Prince Alexius seemed to be quite normal, but gradually his nurses noticed that he was not like other children. When he fell, he bruised

Rasputin

badly. His cuts would not heal as other children's did. It was discovered that he was suffering from the dread disease hemophilia, for which no cure is known. His mother, through whom he had inherited the disease, became frantic with grief and turned to anybody who promised to make her child well.

An ignorant, filthy peasant, who had deserted his own family, and spent his time wandering about the country as a beggar claiming to be a "holy man," was brought to the attention of the royal family, for he said he could work miracle cures. The man's name was Gregory Novykh, but he became known to the world as "Rasputin."

Rasputin soon convinced Alexandra he had cured the little prince—and from that time on the superstitious Empress was completely under his spell.

When the heir to the Austro-Hungarian throne was assassinated on a visit to Sarajevo in 1914, Austria blamed Serbia and declared war. Russia backed Serbia, so Germany backed Austria. Germany then declared war on both Russia and France. Within a week the first World War had begun, a war that would bring death to millions of people and would completely change the Russian way of life.

For several years Russians fought bravely, but there were never enough weapons, ammunition, and food. At one time, soldiers were ordered to the front without weapons; they were told to pick up the guns of those who were killed. Defeat followed defeat. The tsar decided to go to the front himself to lead one of the armies.

While the tsar was with his army, Rasputin had his big chance to become almost the ruler of Russia, so complete was his hold over Empress Alexandra, whom the tsar had unwisely left in charge of the government. Rasputin's power was not broken until he was murdered by several desperate men, close to the royal family, who saw in his death the only hope of saving their country.

By the spring of 1917, Russian morale was shattered. The army had been whipped and the men knew it; millions were wounded or had been taken prisoners of war. On the home front there were strikes, bread lines, mutiny. People were hungry, and rumors were flying in all directions.

In Petrograd, as St. Petersburg had been renamed during the war, factory workers whispered to each other, "The secret police plan to start a riot and will use that as an excuse to kill all of us!"

"No, they plan to starve us first, then shoot when we ask for bread." The word passed from mouth to mouth.

Everyone remained tense and waited for trouble. Then a few small incidents occurred that "triggered" the mighty Russian Revolution. A hungry crowd had gathered in front of some bakery shops in Petrograd and store windows were broken.

The crackle of breaking glass was a signal to the nervous factory workers in nearby buildings. They dropped whatever they were doing and poured into the streets. They milled around, not knowing quite what to do next. The following day, factories were closed. People, by now truly frightened, whispered to each other, "I warned you—the Revolution has come!" They waited, wondering what would happen next.

Soldiers appeared. They fired a few shots and then melted into the crowd. They were seen no more, for their sympathy was with the hungry people rather than with the government.

Nicholas II was asked to abdicate and he did so, in favor of his brother, the Grand Duke Michael. By that time, feeling had grown too strong; the Russian people wanted no more tsars. Many groups opposed the Romanovs, but they could not agree among themselves on what to do next. Alexander Kerensky led a moderate group, some of whom were members of the nobility, while others were of peasant background. Vladimir Ilyich Ulyanov, now offically known as N. Lenin, led a group of hard, professional revolutionists. The Lenin group, which eventually won control, were known at first as "Bolsheviks," the name they had taken in London. Later they came to be called "Communists," a name they have held ever since.

After the tsar's abdication, the royal family were held

captive in their palace. To get needed exercise, they planted a small vegetable garden on the front lawn. One day the tsar, with time hanging heavily on his hands, decided to test the thirteen-year-old tsarevich, for he suspected the boy was not doing as well as he should in his studies. The tsar was so astonished by the boy's ignorance that he declared he would tutor him in history and geography himself, and the empress and the princesses offered to coach him in the subjects they knew best.

This simple "family-style" life, as prisoners in a palace, was not to continue long. Suddenly the royal family were shipped to Ekaterinburg, in Siberia. The following year they were executed, just as a rescuing army approached the city.

Then began a strange tale. It was as if the clock had been turned back to the early seventeenth century, when each of the "false Dmitrys" claimed to be the rightful heir to the Russian throne.

Not long after the tsar and his family were killed, people began to whisper that one of the princesses was still alive. Anastasia had not died with the rest of her family, they said, but had mysteriously been spirited away to recover from her wounds. After a time, girls began to appear all over the world who claimed to be the "true" Anastasia.

Each time a girl made her claim, romantic people the world over hoped her story would prove true. Each time the girl would be asked many questions that the testers thought only a real Russian princess would be able to answer. Some girls failed at once and showed they were impostors, but a few knew most of the answers. One girl was even accepted by the real Anastasia's grandmother. Perhaps the old grandmother was not really deceived by her; no one will ever know.

During the years following the death of the royal family, civil war raged throughout Russia. Some of the most desperate

fighting occurred in cities along the Volga. During this
civil war, many thousands of doctors, lawyers, teachers, mu-
sicians, scientists, and business men fled from their homeland
—escaping as best they could across the borders into Europe.
Others, after unbelievable hardships, made their way across
Siberia to the east and sought refuge in Peking or Shanghai.
Refugees were often called "White Russians." They had no
passports, and faced a bleak future, for they were stateless.
Many of them were helped to a new life by Fridtjof Nansen,
the great Norwegian explorer, who devoted the last years
of his life to their problem.

Families became separated, sometimes never to see each
other again. Now and then one of the millions of tragic sep-
arations had a happy ending, when children were reunited
with their parents.

Tanya, a baby only two years old, was one of the lucky
Russian children. She and her seven-year-old brother were the
children of an officer in the tsar's army. Their mother came
from one of the great landed families near Volgograd.
Tanya's father was killed in the early days of the Revolution,
and his widow fled to Constantinople for she, too, was marked
for death. She left her baby Tanya in the care of her nurse,
and the little boy with his teacher, thinking they would not
be noticed if they were in simple homes.

"When things quiet down, I will come back to my babies,"
she promised, for political revolts were nothing new in Russia.
She did not realize that this was no ordinary uprising, but
the beginning of a great struggle that would go on for years.
There would be no going "back home." The Russia she
knew had disappeared forever.

As months passed, the young Russian mother began to
fear she would never see her children again. Then, as if by
a miracle, she met a man from Holland who asked her to be

his wife. She promised to marry him on condition that he get her children out of Russia. This would have discouraged most men, but not this one. He found someone who had the correct travel documents for the U.S.S.R., and sent him to find the children and arrange for their release. Both children were too young to know that the tired and haggard courier who paid the necessary sum so they could leave the U.S.S.R. was not stealing them, but was taking them to their own mother. And so Tanya and her brother started their long trek to Amsterdam and another life, the little girl screaming and kicking in the courier's arms.

VIII

VOLGA FAMINES

UNFORTUNATELY for farmers the world over, not all years are "good" years. And so it is not surprising that as far back as Russian history is known, there have been occasional "bad years" followed by famines. The old Russian chronicles mention one very bad year in 1024. Another in 1215 was described by the monks in the *Chronicle of Novgorod* in these words:

> O, brothers, then was the trouble; they gave their children into slavery. They dug a public grave and filled it full. O, there was trouble! Corpses in the market place, corpses in the street, corpses in the fields; the dogs could not eat up the men.

Famines continued down through the centuries. Some of the worst occurred in 1601-1603 during the reign of Boris Godunov, and in 1873, 1891-1892, and 1921-1922.

On May 7, 1873 an appeal for aid for the famine victims in villages along the Volga was printed in the *Moscow Gazette*. The article was written by one of Russia's greatest writers, Count Leo Tolstoy, who owned property along the Volga and so knew at first hand the conditions that existed there.

The great famine of 1891-1892 was caused by a rainless summer, followed by a bitterly cold winter. The famine of 1921-1922 had a combination of causes, principally drouth and the loss of manpower. Millions of peasant farmers had lost their lives during the first World War and the years immediately following. The death of these farmers probably reduced planting in 1921 by as much as twenty-five percent.

In spite of the rich farm land that stretched across central Russia, the crop yield under the tsars had been the lowest of any major nation in Europe. Russian peasants continued to farm just as their grandfathers and great-grandfathers had farmed for hundreds of years.

Over eighty-five percent of the Russian people still lived in the country areas at the time of the first World War and most of them lived in poverty. The grain that the Russian tsars had been proudly exporting each year came from the great estates and from a few well-to-do peasants. Although there were a few peasants with their own farm lands and fine farms, poverty and hunger lurked just around the corner for millions of others. Even in the Kuybyshev district, which lies in the fertile, black-soil zone that crosses the central Volga, more than half the peasants were short of grain even in the best years.

The Act of Emancipation that freed the serfs from bondage in 1861 had not brought them prosperity. The amount of land allotted to their country villages, or "communes," was hardly enough to keep them alive, and the problem grew worse each year, for Russians had large families.

With millions of people living close to hunger all the time, with a steadily rising population, and with old-fashioned methods of farming, war conditions, or even the slightest upset in weather, could spell disaster.

When disaster struck, many peasants had to sell their

tools and livestock to buy food. Some even sold their bit of land—if they had any. But once they had "eaten" land and tools, they found themselves in a far worse plight than before, as they no longer had any means of earning a living.

During the Russian Revolution that began in 1917, many of the poor peasants seized the estates of the rich landowners, who, they felt, had oppressed them, and burned the manor houses and barns after dividing the livestock. Once the

Collective farm

Manor house

owner's house, barns, and possessions were gone, the angry
peasants reasoned that the owner himself would never return. This explains why there are today so few manor houses
or other reminders of the estates that once dotted Russia.

Fighting continued for several years after the abdication
of Tsar Nicholas II in 1917. Much of it occurred in the valley
of the Volga with Conservative and Bolshevik (now Communist) armies, Cossacks, and Czechoslovakian forces batt-

ling in all directions. Gradually the Communist forces gained
control of Russia. Although many of the early Communist
leaders clashed with each other over what course to follow,
a plan for a Union of Soviet Socialist Republics took shape,
and Lenin became the first chairman of the Soviet People's
Commissars.

Following hard on the heels of the armies came looters
—desperate gangs of men who plundered and killed. One of
the most daring thieves was Antonov, who centered his attacks on Saratov and the thrifty farms of the Germans whose
ancestors had been invited to settle along the Volga in the
1760's. Antonov made off with grain and thousands of horses
and cattle.

Following behind the armies and the looters came disease
and starvation. In the war-torn land, many people died of
typhus, typhoid, cholera, malaria, or tuberculosis. And everyone—everywhere—was hungry.

Even when people were able to plant crops in those dark
days, there was no way of distributing the life-saving food
to the people. In Volga farm villages, hungry men tried desperately to "stretch" grain by mixing it with straw, weeds,
and bark. Food was even scarcer in Russian cities.

The Communists insisted that the farm villages send more
food to the cities. Well-to-do peasant farmers—or Kulaks as
they were called—balked, and offered many excuses for hold-
ing back their harvest.

"We have sent all we can; we are hungry, too."

"We have only enough grain left for seed; if we give up
our seed we shall have nothing to plant next year."

The Communist authorities were certain that there was
a great deal more food in the villages than the Kulaks would
admit and decided to find it. They appointed "committees"
of poverty-stricken peasants who would know how to go

about hunting for something hidden on a farm. These peasant committees worked in teams with groups of armed factory workers sent out from the cities to bring back the food. The teams had orders to seize all grain they could find hidden.

The searching parties moved from village to village. They tapped walls and floors. They dug. They looked for secret bins. There was not so much as a mound in a field or a pile of junk in a barnyard that was not examined.

Both the Communist leaders who organized the searches and the farmers who defied them were partly right. It turned out that there were hidden stores of grain which the searching teams found and shipped to the hungry cities. And there was also a very real danger of famine, just as the Kulaks had claimed.

At this critical moment, drouth struck. By the autumn of 1921, millions of people in the Volga regions faced not merely hunger but starvation. A quiet hung over the land.

IX

GIVING A HELPING HAND

IT WAS FAR MORE DIFFICULT in the nineteenth century than it now is to help stricken areas—not because people are more kindhearted today, but because the world is better organized to rush aid wherever it is needed.

W. C. Edgar, editor of the flour manufacturers' journal, the *Northwestern Miller*, was the one responsible in 1891 for bringing the Volga famine of that year to American attention. He described the desperate plight of central Russia and appealed for donations of flour and meal.

Although the tsar denied that any part of his realm was starving, he was unable to silence a few Russian noblemen who were doing all they could to relieve the suffering. One of the noblemen was Count Leo Tolstoy, the same Tolstoy who had brought to people's attention the Volga famine of 1873.

Edgar headed a drive in the United States for contributions of flour and meal, and nearly five million pounds had been donated by February 1892. The city of Philadelphia gave so generously that it decided to provide its own ship, the *Indiana*. Another vessel, the *Missouri*, was loaded in Baltimore with gifts from the rest of the United States. Stevedores, harbor pilots, tugboat workers—in fact, everyone who had a part in loading and provisioning the ships—did the job without payment. The *Indiana* and the *Missouri* were soon followed by the *Conemaugh*, the *Tynehead*, and the *Leo*.

A year later, two Russian warships visited New York and Philadelphia in connection with the World's Columbian Exposition held in 1893 in Chicago. The warships brought a message of thanks from the tsar to the American people and

Relief ship *Missouri*

rich gifts of silver for those who had been in charge of the numerous relief drives in the United States. About $700,000 worth of private aid had been sent by the American people to the Russian people during the Volga famine of 1891-92.

In 1921 the West knew nothing at first of the drouth centered in the middle Volga region. When the news began to leak out, it was denied. Then, on June 26, the Communist newspaper *Pravda* stated that twenty-five million people were living in an area seriously affected. On July 11, the patriarch of the Russian Orthodox Church and the writer Maxim Gorky were given permission to appeal for help. Gorky described conditions in his war-torn country and begged the people of Europe and America to send bread and medicine before it was too late.

Many groups in Europe did what they could to help, and so many organizations in the United States offered assistance that an American Relief Administration was set up by Presiden Warren G. Harding, to coordinate and administer the relief program. President Harding asked Herbert Hoover, who later became President of the United States himself, to head the agency. But first the Communist authorities were asked to grant permission for American relief officials to move freely about Russia to supervise the distribution of the food that would be sent from the United States.

Americans gave generously. Twenty-five million dollars were raised through personal contributions. Congress appropriated an additional twenty million dollars and gave the medical supplies "left over" from World War I, which were valued at an additional four million dollars. During the next two years, more than half a million tons of American food, clothing, and medical supplies crossed the Atlantic to Russia.

A staff of two hundred Americans under the direction of Colonel William Haskell accompanied the gifts. This field staff was assisted by about eighty thousand Russians who worked on local committees, usually headed by the village doctor or the schoolmaster.

The work of the Relief Administration was only half over when the food and medical supplies reached Russia. The men still had to get the supplies to the people who needed them. Many Russian harbors were frozen so that ships could not move through the ice-choked waters to unload their cargo. Due to seven years of war conditions, freight cars were hard to locate and trains crawled slowly. Sometimes a train would mysteriously disappear and be "missing" for as much as ten, twenty, or even thirty days! Sometimes, for two weeks or more, no trains would be able to move from railroad yards. Most of the Volga River was frozen in winter and many of the hungry lived in villages that were miles from any transportation.

Before World War I, a third of Russia's freight had traveled on rivers and canals, but by 1921 the war and the Russian Revolution that followed the war had cut the number of river ships from four thousand to two thousand. Many of the twenty-five thousand river barges had been chopped up for fuel, and there were now only fifty-five hundred of them.

In spite of the loss of ships and barges, some means of water transport had to be found, and found quickly, in order to move the grain from the distribution centers of Rybinsk, Gorky, and Volgograd as soon as the ice broke in May. Everything that would float was pressed into service. Some boats traveled over a thousand miles on the Volga and up its tributaries to carry life-saving food closer to hungry or starving villages.

Once the grain had reached a boat landing or a train stop, there was still the job of getting it to remote settlements. Few horses had been able to survive the war years and those that had were now skin and bones. It was often necessary to send oats to feed the animals so they would have enough strength to pull their loads. Russian camels saved the day. They were able to live and keep strong on a diet of "cockle-burs, cactus and thistle"—or so it seemed to the American relief workers.

Men worked with desperate speed, for food had to reach even the most remote villages by sleigh or sled before the spring thaw set in. The Russian workers told the Americans that wagon wheels would be held fast by the glue-like mud of the Russian steppes when the snows melted.

At Volgograd, American corn arrived by train when the ice was still on the river, but before it had all been given out, the weather turned warm and the ice began to crack. This did not stop the daring and courageous Russian peasants. When they could no longer safely cross the thawing Volga with horses, they volunteered to take the grain across on hand sleds. They pushed the sleds in front of them with poles so that they would not add their own weight to that of the loaded sled on the melting ice.

At Lenin's birthplace, Ulyanovsk, more than three thou-sand horses and sleds had come together, from hundreds of little villages, to wait for a train of forty-three cars that had been nearly a month on the way from a Black Sea port.

As the loaded wagons or sleds approached each little farm community, sometimes after two or three hundred miles of travel, peasants streamed out to greet them. Corn got to some of the towns in the Saratov district on Good Friday, which at that time was the start of the greatest Russian festi-val of the whole year, Easter. At the sight of the corn, men and women dropped to their knees and gave thanks as Easter bells pealed from Russian churches.

A year rolled by. When spring arrived in 1923, the ter-

Carrying grain on hand sleds

rible Volga famine was over, except for a few isolated spots. Refugees could still be seen sitting in a jumble of boxes and bundles on railroad station platforms. But this time they were heading back home!

The work of the American Relief Administration was finished, and the top officials prepared to leave for the United States after having spent two years in Russia. The Council of People's Commissars, as the new Communist governing body in Russia was called, gave a farewell dinner in their honor in Moscow. The ceremonies concluded with the presentation of a hand-printed and elaborately decorated scroll. On this beautiful scroll the leaders of the Communist government gave their official thanks for a helping hand.

RESOLUTION OF THE SOVIET
OF PEOPLE'S COMMISSARS

In the trying hour of a great and overwhelming disaster, the people of the United States, represented by the A.R.A., responded to the needs of the population, already exhausted by intervention and blockade, in the famine-stricken parts of Russia and Federated Republics.

Unselfishly, the A.R.A. came to the aid of the people and organized on a broad scale the supply and distribution of food products and other articles of prime necessity.

Due to the enormous and entirely disinterested efforts of the A.R.A., millions of people of all ages were saved from death, and entire districts and even cities were saved from the horrible catastrophe which threatened them.

Now when the famine is over and the colos-

ПОСТАНОВЛЕНИЕ СОВЕТА НАРОДНЫХ КОМИССАРОВ

В тяжелую годину огромного стихийного бедствия американский народ в лице АРА откликнулся на нужды измученного интервенцией и блокадой населения пораженных голодом областей России и Союзных Республик и пришел самоотверженно ему на помощь, организовав в широком масштабе подвоз и распределение продуктов и других предметов первой необходимости. Благодаря громадным, совершенно бескорыстным усилиям АРА миллионы людей всех возрастов были спасены от смерти и целые селения и даже города уцелели от грозившей им страшной катастрофы. В настоящее время, когда с прекращением голода грандиозная работа АРА приходит к концу, Совнарком от имени спасенных миллионов и всего трудящегося народа Советской России и Союзных Республик считает своим долгом перед лицом всего мира выразить этой организации, ее главе Герберту Гуверу, представителю в России полковнику Хаскелю и всем ее сотрудникам свою глубочайшую благодарность и заявить, что народы, населяющие Союз Советских Социалистических Республик, никогда не забудут оказанной им американским народом через АРА помощи, усматривая в ней залог будущей дружбы обоих народов.

Зам. председателя Совета
Народных Комиссаров

Управляющий делами Совета
Народных Комиссаров

Секретарь Совета
Народных Комиссаров

Москва Кремль июль 1923 г.

sal work of the A.R.A. comes to a close, the Soviet of People's Commissars, in the name of the millions of people saved and in the name of all the working people of Soviet Russia and the Federated Republics, counts it a duty to express before the whole world its deepest thanks to this organization, to its leader, Herbert Hoover, to its representative in Russia, Colonel Haskell, and to all its workers, and to declare that the people inhabiting the Union of Soviet Socialist Republics will never forget the help given them by the American people, through the A.R.A., seeing in it a pledge of the future friendship of the two nations.

L. Kamenev,
Acting President of the Council of
People's Commissars

N. Gorbunov,
Chief of the Administrative Dept. of
the Council of People's Commissars

L. Fotieva,
Secretary of the Council of
People's Commissars
Moscow, Kremlin
July 10, 1923

X

THE "NEW" VOLGA

TODAY A TRIP down the busy, muddy Volga on one of the new Russian cruise ships will give a traveler more than a Russian holiday. It will introduce the "new" industrial Volga and give, at the same time, insight into more than a thousand years of changing history and customs.

Long before man invented railroads, camel caravans camped at spots along the Volga. Today many of the important cities along the river mark the spot where the caravan route once crossed.

When Russian railroads were first built, they were portages linking waterways, for rivers have always been highways across the great plains of eastern Europe and Siberia. One of the earliest Russian railroads was the short Kalach-Tsaritsyn Line which connected the Volga with the Don.

As an agricultural nation, Russia had to import many of the manufactured things it needed—or do without them. One of the great tasks confronting the Communists, when they came into power, was the turning of an agricultural nation into an economically independent one. Factories, power plants, steel mills, and oil refineries had to be built. Chemical and building industries had to be developed.

The Communist government found, as it tried to create

75

Camel caravan

an industrial nation almost overnight, that the people's lack of education created many problems. Millions of Russians who had never before had a chance to go to school had to be trained so they could take part in the new program.

In December 1920, the Eighth Congress of Soviets adopted a state plan for the electrification of Russia, known as the GOELRO Plan, its initials in Russian. This was the first Soviet economic program. The electrification scheme called for a single high-voltage transmission network that would link, in one power system, all of the U.S.S.R. that lies in **Europe.**

In 1928 the Communists launched the first of a series of Five-Year Plans to develop their country, setting a definite "goal" for each period. Before World War II, there was no reason to suspect that the middle Volga region would become the fastest growing section in the U.S.S.R. in a few years. Although oil had been discovered between the Ural Mountains and the Volga River in 1929, 87% of all Soviet oil still was coming from the Caucasus in 1940 and the Russians still looked on the Caucasus as their most important source of oil.

World War II started the development of the middle Volga. When Moscow was under siege, and when it looked

Steel mill

as if the city might be captured by the German army, the central government was moved from Moscow to Kuybyshev which seemed at that time a remote and comparatively safe place. Factories and important industries were also moved, piece by piece, to the Volga valley and set up where they would be safe from attack.

In 1960 the Volga-Ural oil deposits, now known to stretch from Volgograd to Perm, produced more than 70% of the total oil output of the U.S.S.R. The goal for 1965 was put at 73%. It is now believed that about 80% of the total oil reserves of the Soviet Union are located here. (See map, page 79.)

The U.S.S.R. has already nosed out Venezuela as number two producer of oil—and is second only to the United States. Oil and natural gas have brought rapid change to many cities and towns between Kazan and Volgograd. Refineries and factories have sprung up overnight, and pipe and gas lines are being laid for hundreds of miles to reach distant cities in the U.S.S.R. and its satellites.

Even the shape of the Volga is changing. No longer is the river allowed to flood in the spring and then dry up in the fall until sand bars show. The Volga has now become a "ladder" that Russian engineers have learned to control through a complicated system of reservoirs, dams, spillways, floodgates, sluices, pumping and power stations. There are already dams at Ivankovo, Uglich, Rybinsk, Gorodets, Kuybyshev and Volgograd that create great bulges—man-made lakes where millions of gallons of water are impounded to feed hydroelectric stations. From the air these reservoirs make the Volga look like a writhing snake that has swallowed more than it can digest!

In 1957, when the Lenin Hydroelectric Station near Kuybyshev began to operate at full capacity, it was the world's

Volga-Ural oil-producing area first discovered in 1929. Nearly
three-quarters of the Soviet oil comes from the central tinted area
of the map: in 1960 the area produced 70% of all the oil in the
U.S.S.R.; in 1965, the area will produce 73% of all the oil in
the U.S.S.R.

largest power station, but within three years the even larger Volgograd Hydroelectric Station was finished. When its twenty-one turbo-generators went into operation on December 9, 1960, the once sluggish Volga became wide and rough. Its gray-green waters slapped hard against the immense walls of concrete that held them back. The river now drops in a 110-foot waterfall to the waiting vanes of the turbines. When Russian engineers throw the switch, the "new" Volga suddenly becomes a modern giant, hard at work.

XI

VOLGA BOATMEN OF LONG AGO

IN SPITE OF THE CHANGES that are being made in the river, thousands of logs are still floated down the Volga each year from the great forests of the north. The logs are tied so as to form "rafts" and on each raft there is a little log cabin in which the raftmen live during the voyage. When the logs reach the treeless lower Volga and are sold, the little hut is sold too, and becomes somebody's home. To anyone who had not seen the huts floating down the river in this strange manner, it is puzzling to find log cabins on desert steppes where there is not a tree in sight!

The raftmen, once the voyage is finished, return to the wooded north by train, to start another trip down the Volga.

Before World War I, life on the Volga River was very different from what it is today. A great many more men earned a living on the river and its tributaries then. They were the Volga "boatmen" about whom dozens of songs and stories have been written. People all over the world—even those who had no idea where the Volga River was—knew the *Song of the Volga Boatmen,* by Nikolay Alexeyevich Nekrasov.

Log cabins on rafts

Go down to the Volga,
That great Russian River
O'er whose waters
A groaning doth go.

The Burlaks are hauling
With a sigh and a shiver
Towing and tugging
And chanting "Heave-Ho!"

Old-time Volga boatmen lived a hard life, for they were
"roustabouts"—only one step above tramps. In years gone

by, their job was to pull tow ropes on barges. They worked and slept on their rafts and barges, and stopped at villages along the way to buy food.

At night, daring village boys would sneak down to the boatmen's camps on the banks of the Volga and listen wide-eyed to tall tales of adventure.

"I heard a strange story the other day," one boatman would begin, giving the campfire a poke. "And the person who told me swore by our Little Mother that it is true. Do you remember that old crone who used to glare at us each time we passed Sosnovka? THAT WOMAN WAS A WITCH." Then, glancing around the circle to make sure he had the attention of everyone, he would begin his gory tale.

Last week the old crone of Sosnovka breathed her last. But before she died, she summoned her daughter to her.

"Mind you listen carefully," the crone said. "When I'm dead, do not wash my body with warm water. Instead fill a cauldron and make it boil. Then scald me all over."

After she had finished speaking, the old crone lay back in her bed and died. Her daughter ran to the neighbors—just as she should—to beg them to help her wash the old woman. Her own child she left alone in the cottage—alone with the corpse.

"And then do you know what happened?" Here the Volga boatman would turn to his gaping audience.

Then all of a sudden there came out from under the stove two demons—one big; one small. They scurried over to that old dead witch—for that's what she was—never once noticing the child.

The big one grabbed the witch by the feet and gave her a terrible yank, ripping her skin right off in one big pull! Then he turned to the little demon and said, "You can have her flesh but take it under the stove."

So the little demon flung his arms round his prize and dragged it out of sight. Now nothing was left of that old witch but skin and into that skin the big demon crawled! Then he lay down exactly in the spot where she had been lying.

After a bit the old crone's daughter returned, bringing six women with her, and they set about preparing the corpse as is the custom.

"Why did they pull off Granny's skin?" asked the child, coming out from a dark corner.

"Hold your tongue, naughty child," her mother warned. Then she fetched a big cauldron, just as she had been told by the old crone to do. She filled it with water, and put it on the fire to boil.

When the water was boiling furiously, the women heaved the old crone onto a trough. Then all six

Volga boatmen

took hold of the cauldron, carried it to the trough, and dumped it over her.

When that boiling water struck the old demon who had crawled into the skin, he couldn't stand it. With one leap he was out of the trough and through the door. Whoosh! He was gone—skin and all!

"Don't scare the boys—" another boatman would be sure to interrupt with a wink. "Can't you see that they are beginning to look into every shadow?"

Then, keeping a perfectly straight face, he would raise his own voice so that all would hear. "As we were buying to-night's food in the village, there was someone—someone sitting here before me—who was so hungry he could not wait. He bought himself a large bun and gulped it down. Still hungry, he bought a second bun and ate it. His hunger still gnawing on him like a wolf, he bought still a third bun and ate it, too. When three big, fat buns had failed to satisfy his

mighty appetite, he bought pretzels. After swallowing a pretzel he was no longer hungry.

"Suddenly I saw him clap his hand to his head and wail, 'What a fool I am! Why did I waste my precious kopecks buying buns? I should have eaten that pretzel in the first place!'"

As soon as the good-natured laughter around the campfire had died down, another storyteller would begin a long tale, less gruesome than the first.

Thatched log hut with carved window frame

Volga boatmen in motor-driven tugs

Once upon a time, the Volga and Dvina and Dnieper were not rivers at all but living people. In those days the Dnieper was a boy; the Volga and Dvina were his sisters. They were left orphans at an early age without so much as one crust of bread so that they must work far beyond their strength to keep from starving . . .

Sometimes a boy who listened open-mouthed to these old Russian folktales "forgot" to go home after the story was done. The life of a Volga boatman seemed to him the only way to a life of adventure.

The little villages from which the boys came were often no more than a dozen low, thatched, log huts—unpainted and weatherbeaten. But often their carved window frames were painted a bright blue or red, providing the only touch of color.

Today even these little river communities, far from industrial centers, have changed. They have become either Soviet *Kolkhozes* (collective farms) or *Sovkhozes* (government-owned farms where peasants work as people do in a factory). No longer are there the beckoning campfires of roustabout boatmen. Now the Volga boatmen, who once were "towing and tugging and chanting 'heave-ho,'" work on motor-driven tugs that ply up and down the Volga. They wave as they chug by.

XII

VOLGA VACATION

EVERY YEAR nearly five million Russians take the Volga cruise vacation. Often the river holiday is arranged by a trade union. Many of the cruise ships start at Moscow and travel up the Moscow Canal to the Volga. (See map, page 92.)

Russian tourists, lining the rails of the cruise ship, are bundled up in sweaters, even in summer, for the weather often is cool. The climate along the upper Volga is like that of southern Canada.

As mentioned before, there is a great deal that is "old" and a great deal that is "new" to be seen on a Volga River cruise. Here and there bell towers and onion-shaped domes of old churches appear. Horse-drawn carts raise clouds of dust that can be seen billowing along rutted country roads that connect drab little villages.

Not many miles from these symbols of "old" Russia are the symbols of the "new" U.S.S.R.—row after row of tall apartment buildings that house the thousands of new urban workers and, near the workers' homes, the new factories, mills, and power plants in which they earn a living. At times one catches a glimpse of schools, camps, parks, and sports stadiums.

A cruise starting from Moscow will miss Kalinin, the

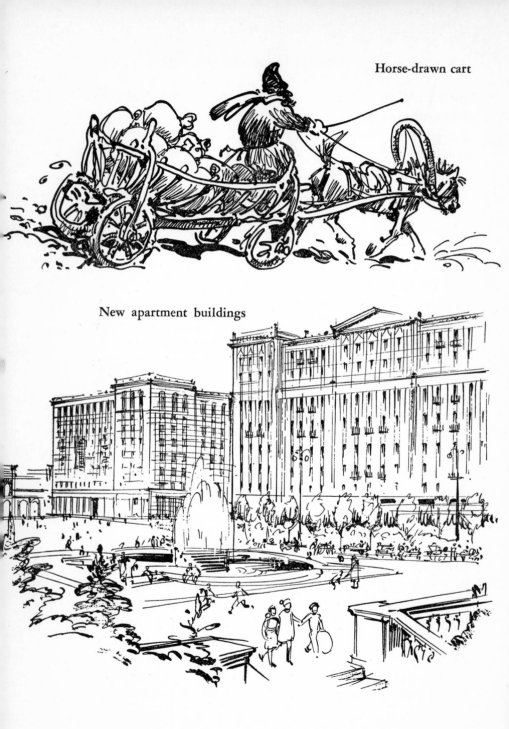

Horse-drawn cart

New apartment buildings

historic old city of Tver, as it was previously called. From the thirteenth to the fifteenth centuries Tver was Moscow's greatest rival. Today, as Kalinin, it is a factory town and manufactures textiles and railway cars. Cruise ships from Moscow enter the Volga at Ivankovo which is a little below Kalinin.

On a Volga cruise, Russian tourists can relive much of their country's rich history—a history still little known outside the U.S.S.R. At Uglich, tourists stream ashore to see with their own eyes one gruesome bit of Russia's story. Here it was that Boris Godunov, more than 350 years ago, took terrible revenge on the village that accused him of plotting little Prince Dmitry's death during the "Time of Troubles." Even the church bell that had been rung as a warning is said to have been taken down and "exiled."

Passing from the Rybinsk Reservoir, the impounded waters of which help to make possible the deep-water canal route to Moscow today, the cruise ship comes to the city of Rybinsk, known for its shipbuilding and woodworking industry.

Next, ancient Yaroslavl comes into view. It was one of the earliest settlements on the Volga and was named in honor of Yaroslav the Wise. During the 1930's it became the synthetic rubber center of the U.S.S.R., as Akron is in the United States. It is probably the most highly industrialized city in the whole Soviet Union, with sixty percent of its people working in factories.

A little farther downstream is Kostroma, built in the Middle Ages as a fort to guard against Tatar attack. It was at Ipatev Monastery in Kostroma that Michael Romanov received the allegiance of nobles and clergy in 1613, becoming the first of the Romanov dynasty that would rule Russia with an iron hand until 1917. Today Kostroma is the

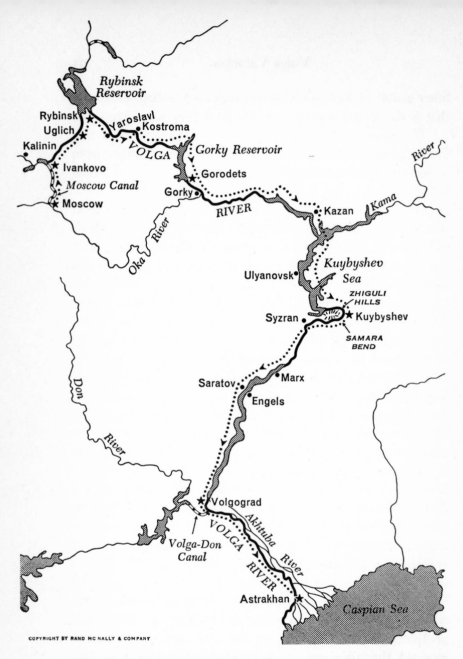

Map showing the route of the cruise on the Volga from Moscow to Astrakhan. This route is shown by the line of arrows. Those places marked with a star are dams and power stations.

linen center of the U.S.S.R., for it is in the part of Russia that is the largest producer of flax in the world.

The ship passes many small settlements and larger industrial centers as it approaches Gorky at the junction of the Volga and Oka rivers. Gorky is the "Detroit" of the Soviet Union. In 1932, the Russians asked Henry Ford to send engineers to Gorky to help set up an automobile factory. The plant that Ford helped build now produces the *Zim*. Much of the heavy Volga traffic—the steady stream of barges moving to and fro on the river—either begins or ends in this great industrial city.

Under its old name, Nizhny Novgorod, Gorky had a romantic past, and was known throughout the eastern world for the gigantic and colorful bazaar held there for two months of each year. In row upon row of solid brick stalls, treasures were exhibited that had come by camel caravan, by barge, wagon, or train. There were Persian and Chinese carpets, tea, dried fish, and salted cucumbers, furs, and precious stones. There were perfumes, silverware, linen, and holy images. Thousands of items were spread out for Russian merchants to examine and purchase. Merchants came from all over Russia to select their wares for the coming year. Chinese, Persian, Greek, Turkish, and German dealers worked feverishly selling the products they had brought from their homelands, and gestured wildly as they tried to make themselves understood in a dozen different languages.

Today all is changed, and the great Nizhny Novgorod Fair is only a memory, for the Communist government does not permit private industry. The solidly built old stalls have been turned into homes. Even the old name of the city is gone—changed to Gorky to honor the writer Maxim Gorky.

Beyond Gorky the Volga leaves the densely populated central industrial region and heads toward the southeast.

Bazaar in Nizhny Novgorod

Now the ship is entering the long stretch of the Volga that is known to the Russian people as the *Povolzhye*. This word means "along the Volga," but it means much more than that to the Russian tourists. It has a special meaning, much as the expressions going to the "Coast," the "Midwest," or "back East" have for Americans.

Kazan, the next stop on the cruise, still shows its oriental beginning. For many years it was a Tatar stronghold and until recent times was a strongly Mohammedan city. Kazan became a great center of learning, and both Tolstoy and Lenin journeyed there to attend the university. In 1956 Kazan was threatened by the Kuybyshev Sea—as the water piling up above the great power station at Kuybyshev is now called. Thick dikes have had to be built to keep Kazan from being "drowned."

The next stop on the cruise is the Communist shrine, Ulyanovsk, the birthplace of Lenin. At the time Lenin was

Kazan today

born, the city was known as Simbirsk. The name was not changed until 1923, when it was renamed to honor Lenin's true name, Ulyanov.

Below Ulyanovsk, at the point where the Volga swings around the Zhiguli Hills, Kuybyshev stretches out on the flat eastern shore. Kuybyshev is about the size of Milwaukee or Boston. Many years ago it was the charming, sleepy, provincial city, Samara. Well-to-do families, who owned estates nearby, kept town houses in Samara, for it lies in the heart of one of the great Russian grain-producing regions.

Samara fought desperately to hold out against the Bolshevik forces in 1918. Nevetheless, it was the city selected by the Communists twenty-three years later during the second World War, to be the new capital of the U.S.S.R. if Moscow had to be abandoned to the advancing German army. Part of the reason may be that Kuybyshev—to use its present name —lies almost as far east as Teheran, the capital of Iran.

Under Communism, Kuybyshev has grown to be a Soviet "Pittsburgh." In addition to mills, factories, and food-processing plants, it is rapidly becoming the center of activities for the rich Volga-Ural oil fields. Syzran, which is across the Volga on the high, western side, and about fifty miles below Kuybyshev, is the other great refining center for Volga oil.

Beyond the Samara Bend, eagle-eyed tourists notice a change in vegetation. It is the same kind of change travelers see when they drive from Chicago to Denver. Gradually, rich farm land becomes drier in appearance; grain gives way to meat; and farms become ranches.

When the cruise ship reaches Volgograd, which stretches out for more than thirty-five miles along the high western bank of the river, eager tourists stream ashore. Volgograd is the new name for Stalingrad—which was called Tsaritsyn for hundreds of years before it became Stalingrad in 1925.

As Stalingrad, it became one of the five "Hero Cities" of the U.S.S.R. in World War II.

To understand the place Volgograd—or Stalingrad—holds in the hearts of the Russian people, one must turn back to the winter of 1941:

Adolf Hitler had invaded the U.S.S.R. on June 22, 1941 in spite of the fact that he had signed a non-aggression treaty with the Communist government in August 1939. At first Hitler was successful, and pushed deep into Russia. By October he boasted that his troops already held a slice of Russia larger than all of Germany was in 1933. However, his generals were not able to take Leningrad or Moscow that autumn, and the German army was strung out on a thousand-mile front when winter set in.

Hitler ordered his generals to stand firm, assuring them that in the spring it would be an easy matter to take Russia. It was a winter of great suffering for the German forces, who had brought no winter clothing. Germany is cold in winter, but a German winter, they discovered, is mild in comparison with a Russian winter.

When the spring of 1942 finally arrived, part of the German force pushed east toward Stalingrad and the Volga, part swung south toward the oil fields of the Caucasus. Hitler's army might have won on one or the other front, but his supply line was too long to take care of two fronts deep in enemy territory. Although Hitler had been a house painter by trade, he felt that he knew more about military matters than his generals did, and ordered them to take Stalingrad at all costs. He paid no attention to the problem of supplies and reinforcements. All he could think of was cutting the Volga "life line"—which he likened to a man's jugular vein.

The people of Stalingrad swore they would never let the Germans capture the city and cross the Volga. They swore to defend the city to the last man if need be. And so from September 13, 1942 until January 31, 1943 the siege of Stalingrad continued, with German guns trained on the city and Germans and Russians fighting in hand-to-hand combat from street to street, from house to house, and from room to room—as long as there were rooms left through which to dodge.

The Russians refused to give up. They fought bravely on and slowly began to get the upper hand. When a Soviet counter-attack began, Hitler refused to let the German general in command retreat to save his men. Now the German army was in a desperate plight. No reinforcements came to its rescue; even German planes could not get through.

Tighter and tighter the Communists drew the net, like fishermen pulling in a catch. By January 17, the Germans were trapped in an area that measured only four by eight miles. By February 2, the five-month-long battle was over. The Communists took prisoner all who were left alive in the German army. Stalingrad was destroyed, but so were Hitler's plans for conquering the U.S.S.R.

There are historical treasures in the Volgograd Museum that have as much interest for American as for Soviet citizens. One is a scroll, dated May 17, 1944, given by Franklin D. Roosevelt, then President of the United States, to honor the people of Stalingrad for their heroic defense of their city. Here, too, is the jeweled sword that King George VI of England sent with his congratulations.

Today Volgograd is a completely new city, rebuilt on the ruins of the old.

At the entrance to the Volga-Don Canal, a little below the city, the towering statue of Josef Stalin was once a familiar landmark. This costly statue became a "white elephant" when

One of the Volgograd statues of Josef Stalin, no longer standing

Stalin ceased to be one of the Communist heroes, and it was removed in 1961.

Tourists watching the shore notice many patches of irrigated land below Volgograd. Melons, fruit, cotton, and rice thrive here, if the parched earth of the lower Volga flood-plain is watered.

The little villages along the Volga have been changing, too. No longer can log huts be seen scattered here and there along a single street. As trees gave way to treeless steppes, the little log cabins gave way to dun-colored, rounded "igloos" of adobe that seem to hug the earth.

Often the floor of a little adobe hut is scooped out two or three feet below the earth's surface to give the family

Adobe "igloo"

living in it greater protection from the winter winds. The lower stretches of the Volga freeze over in winter, although the river shimmers with heat in summer.

Below Volgograd, the Volga drops below sea level; when it reaches Astrakhan, it will be more than seventy feet below.

The old Tatar stronghold of Astrakhan is now an important fishing and shipping center where thousands of Volga river boats and barges discharge cargoes of grain, timber, and goods from up river and load salt, oil, fruit, cotton, fish, and caviar for the long journey north.

Russians are proud of their rich, black caviar—a delicacy that comes from the lower Volga and the Caspian, the Aral, and the Black Seas. Black caviar is the roe of sturgeon; red caviar the eggs of salmon. In order to have an unending supply of caviar, Soviet scientists have built many fish farms along the lower Volga.

Some of the cruise passengers visit the fish farms and watch the workers bring ashore the great sturgeon, four to seven feet long. These men are no ordinary fishermen, for they must be especially careful not to injure their catch. Gently they lift each fish from the net in which it was caught and place it in a tank mounted on a truck. Then the truck is driven as carefully as possible from shore to fish farm.

The next job is a hard one: the roe must be removed unharmed from the mother fish. The eggs are then placed in incubator tanks and fertilized with milt from male sturgeons. The roe—by this time "living" caviar—must remain in the tanks for from eight to ten days at a temperature of 70 degrees Fahrenheit. It is then moved to larger tanks for twenty more days before it is put in outdoor pools for still another twenty days. By the time the tiny sturgeon are about fifty days old, they are ready to be released in rivers and inland

Unloading a catch of sturgeon

seas. If all goes well, many of them will grow up to produce more caviar.

* * * * * * * * *

Astrakhan is the turning point in the Volga cruise and the ship starts back to Moscow. In a little over a week it will be time to say goodby to the mighty and ever-changing Volga and to the Russian tourists who have shared their history and their holiday.

Volga cruise ship

BIBLIOGRAPHY

WHEN DOING RESEARCH for *The Volga: Lifeline of Russia*, the author drew on material gleaned from countless sources. Much of this material would be very difficult reading for the boys and girls for whom *The Volga* is written. Nevertheless, a few suggestions are offered for those who would like to read some of these adult books.

Charques, R. D. *A Short History of Russia*. Dutton, 1956.
Clarkson, J. D. *A History of Russia*. Random, 1961.
Harcave, Sidney. *Russia: A History*. Lippincott, 1959.
Kirchner, Walter. *A History of Russia*. Barnes & Noble, 1963.
Pares, Bernard, *History of Russia*. Knopf, 1960.
Riasanovsky, N. V. *A History of Russia*. Oxford University Press, 1963.
Walsh, W. B. *Russia and the Soviet Union: A Modern History*. University of Michigan Press, 1958.

In order to build up a picture of the past, and to go more deeply into some of the incidents covered briefly in *The Volga*, a few highly specialized references are added to our list. Some of the books are long out of print and are available only in larger libraries.

American Heritage, August, 1960. (The article "Bread Upon the Waters" includes information on the Volga famine of 1891–92.)

Fisher, H. H. *The Famine in Soviet Russia, 1919–1923; the Operations of the American Relief Administration.* Macmillan, 1927 (o.p.) and Stanford University, Hoover Inst., 1935. (A documented study based on material in the American Relief Administration archives.)

Gilmore, Eddy. *After the Cossacks Burned Down the "Y".* Farrar, Straus, 1964. (Pulitzer prize-winning journalist "covers" the twentieth anniversary celebration of the Battle of Stalingrad.)

Miller, Wright. *Russians as People.* Dutton, 1960. (One of the best descriptions of the Russian people and Russian countryside.)

Narishkin-Kurakin, Elizabeth. *Under Three Tsars; the Memoirs of the Lady-in-Waiting.* Dutton, 1931 (o.p.). (Eyewitness report on life of the Romanovs.)

Stoddard, C. A. *Across Russia from the Baltic to the Danube.* Scribner, 1891 (o.p.). (Vivid description of the fair at Nizhny-Novgorod during the 19th century.)

Tolstoy, Leo. *Fables and Fairy Tales.* New American Library, 1962. (Most of these fables and fairy tales were drawn from Tolstoy's "primers"—books prepared for peasants who were learning to read. Others were drawn from stories written by Tolstoy to raise funds for the 1891–92 famine relief and for a 1903 pogrom relief. "Three Rolls and a Pretzel" appeared in Tolstoy's *Second Reader,* published in 1872.)

Walsh, Warren B., comp. and ed. *Readings in Russian History from Ancient Times to the Post-Stalin Era;* fourth edition. 3 vol. Syracuse University Press, 1963. (With the publication of these 205 selections, two-thirds of which are primary source material, the reader is given access to information in English previously found only in universities, often only in the Russian language.)

INDEX

Printed in U.S.A.

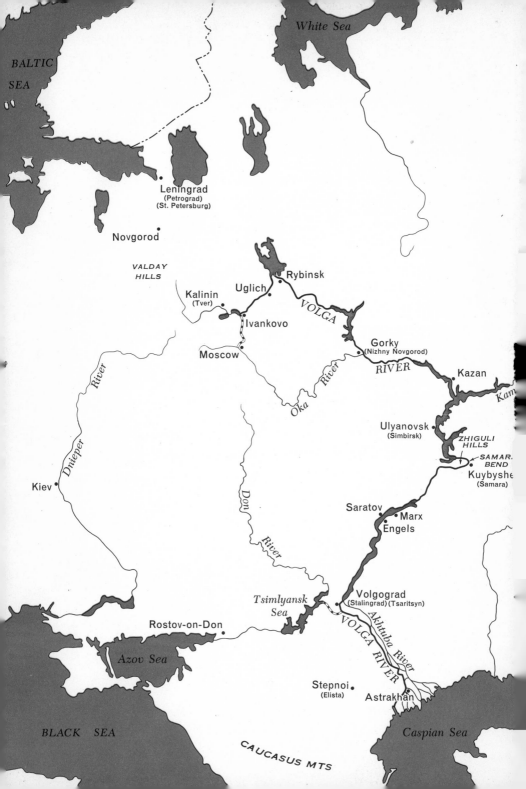